PHOTOGRAPHY

MEDIA WORKSHOP

PHOTOGRAPHY

Take Your Best Shot

*Terri
Morgan
&
Shmuel
Thaler*

LERNER PUBLICATIONS COMPANY
MINNEAPOLIS

*All words that appear in **bold** type are defined in a glossary that begins on page 71.*

This book is available in two editions:
Library binding by Lerner Publications Company
Soft cover by First Avenue Editions
241 First Avenue North/Minneapolis, MN 55401
ISBN 0-8225-2302-7 (lib. bdg.)/ISBN 0-8225-9605-9 (pbk.)

Morgan, Terri.
    Photography : take your best shot / text and photographs by Terri Morgan and Shmuel Thaler.
        p.   cm.
    Includes index.
    Summary: A practical guide to photographic technique, providing information on composition, lighting, special effects, color and black-and-white photographs, equipment, darkroom skills, and careers in photography.
    ISBN 0-8225-2302-7
    1. Photography.—Juvenile literature. [1. Photography.]
    I. Thaler, Shmuel. II. Title.
TR146.M627   1991
771-dc20   90-27054
                                                            CIP
Manufactured in the United States of America   AC

1 2 3 4 5 6 7 8 9 10 00 99 98 97 96 95 94 93 92 91

Contents

Chapter One
THE CAMERA: HOW IT WORKS. 7

Chapter Two
YOUR EQUIPMENT. 11

Chapter Three
COMPOSITION: CREATING GOOD PICTURES. . 21

Chapter Four
PHOTOGRAPHY AND LIGHT. 31

Chapter Five
CAPTURING THE ACTION. 37

Chapter Six
PORTRAITS. 39

Chapter Seven
PHOTOGRAPHING ANIMALS. 43

Chapter Eight
LANDSCAPES AND CITYSCAPES. 47

Chapter Nine
COLOR. 51

Chapter Ten
BLACK AND WHITE. 55

Chapter Eleven
SPECIAL EFFECTS. 57

Chapter Twelve
IN THE DARKROOM. 61

Chapter Thirteen
DISPLAYING YOUR WORK. 65

Chapter Fourteen
CAREERS IN PHOTOGRAPHY. 69

Glossary. 71

Index. 72

Before you can go out and take stunning photographs, you must first learn what all the rings, knobs, and buttons on your camera do and how they work.

Chapter One

THE CAMERA: HOW IT WORKS

Many cameras, such as the one shown, *above*, have a viewfinder that is off to one side of the lens. Single-lens reflex cameras, *below*, use a system with a mirror, focusing screen, and prism to reflect into the viewfinder almost exactly what the lens shows.

All cameras—from the simplest to the most complex—have essential similarities. They are all lighttight boxes. Every camera has a hole, called an **aperture**, on one side to let in light. A **lens** is usually attached to this side. On the other side is a place to hold film.

Viewing Systems

All cameras also have some kind of a **viewfinder**, which allows you to see, more or less, what your film will record. Different cameras, however, use different kinds of viewing systems.

Single-lens reflex cameras, usually called SLRs, use a mirror and prism to allow you to look through the viewfinder to see what the lens sees. "Point-and-shoot" cameras (which require only that you aim at a subject, then push a button), box cameras, instant cameras, and most simple cameras are fitted with a viewfinder. These viewfinders are usually positioned above the lens and off to one side.

Before taking photographs with a manual SLR camera, you must set (1) the shutter speed and (2) the aperture, as well as (3) focus the lens.

If you use one of these cameras, you will get a view that is slightly different from what the camera lens sees.

Focusing Systems

To take good pictures, you must be able to **focus** on your subject. Early cameras and modern point-and-shoot cameras have lenses that are set at a fixed distance from the film. Many cameras, however, have adjustable-focus lenses. Some cameras focus automatically, while others have to be focused by the photographer.

Shutter Systems

Another thing all cameras have in common is a shutter system. A **shutter** is located between the film and the lens, and it opens and closes to control the amount of light that reaches the film. Most 35-millimeter (35mm) cameras have a shutter speed ring or knob, which you can adjust to increase or decrease the length of time the shutter stays open. This ring is usually situated on top of the camera.

Shutter speeds actually represent fractions of a second. The shutter speed

Lenses

Another thing that all cameras have in common is a lens. Lenses gather the light that is recorded on the film. We'll discuss lenses more thoroughly in the next chapter.

Apertures

All cameras have an aperture to allow light to reach the film. The size of the aperture usually can be adjusted.

In most cameras, the aperture is controlled by the **diaphragm**, a set of thin metal plates built into the lens. These plates overlap to form a circle. When you move the aperture ring on the outside of the lens, the hole formed by the diaphragm becomes either larger or smaller. By adjusting the aperture, you can control the amount of light reaching the film.

A set of numbers, called **f-stops**, are used to measure aperture settings. F-stop scales are standard on all interchangeable lenses. On many lenses, f-16 is the smallest opening and lets in the least amount of light. F-11, the next smallest opening, lets in twice the amount of light. F-stops are scaled so that each one lets in twice as much light as the one following it.

You can shoot the same scene with a variety of aperture settings, as long as you adjust the shutter speed accordingly. As you increase the amount of light in an **exposure** by one f-stop, you must decrease the amount of time by one f-stop to compensate. In many automatic cameras this is done for you.

All five of these systems or elements— viewing, focusing, shutters, lenses, and apertures—aren't very useful or significant individually. But together, working as one unit, they combine to allow a camera to function.

500, for example, stands for 1/500th of a second. Likewise, 250 means 1/250th of a second. Since 1/500th of a second is half the time as 1/250th of a second, the faster setting lets in half as much light. Each shutter speed number represents a setting that lets in half as much light as the one before it.

The slowest shutter speed on many cameras is 1, or one second. The setting that follows is "B," which stands for bulb—short for flashbulb. When the shutter is set on bulb, it will remain open for the entire time the shutter button is depressed.

Chapter Two

YOUR EQUIPMENT

Lenses for SLR cameras, *opposite*, come in a variety of sizes, for almost every purpose. Most serious amateur and many professional photographers use SLR cameras because of their versatility.

Learning how to use your equipment and becoming comfortable with it will give you a great start on capturing good images. Once you have mastered your equipment, you can spend more time setting up your shot and waiting for the right moment to take your photograph.

Cameras

There are many different types of cameras, each designed for different uses. One of the most popular types is the single-lens reflex. SLR cameras, which usually create negatives that are about 35 millimeters wide, get their name because of their unique viewing system. A mirror and prism arrangement allows you to look in the viewfinder and see what the lens sees.

Many SLR cameras have an automatic feature that sets the focus, aperture, and shutter speed for you. Most of these programmable cameras have an override feature that allows you to adjust the camera manually as well. Some other SLR cameras are entirely manual.

One reason SLR cameras are so popular is that their lenses can be changed quickly and easily. Just as popular are the point-and-shoot cameras, which also use 35mm film cassettes. Most of these cameras focus and set the exposure automatically.

Many of the point-and-shoot cameras have fixed lenses, which do not allow any focusing. Some have zoom lenses built in and flashes that pop up. Most point-and-shoot cameras employ a viewing system that is separate from the lens. They see a similar, but not identical, view as the lens. Although not as versatile as SLR cameras, point-and-shoot cameras are lighter, easier to use, and often less expensive.

These four photographs, all shot from the same spot, illustrate the differences in focal lengths. A 28mm lens (1) is a wide-angle lens that can take in a substantial part of the scene. A 50mm lens (2) is a standard lens that takes in less of the view.

Instant-print cameras, such as those made by the Polaroid Corporation, are usually larger than 35mm cameras and generally have a fixed lens or an automatic focus lens, as well as a fixed exposure time. The biggest advantage is that they use a special type of film that produces a print within seconds.

Small, inexpensive 110 cameras, which fit into a pocket, usually allow no adjustments. They are easy to use and easy to load. The 110 film comes in cartridges that drop neatly into the back of the camera. You will not have to thread the tail end of the film, called the leader, when loading the camera, nor will you have to rewind the film when you have used it up.

The main drawback of 110 cameras is that the negative they produce is very small. This limits the size and quality of the final print. When enlarged above snapshot size, the images are fuzzy and the color is usually washed out.

There are also inexpensive cameras that are designed to be used once and then thrown away. These disposable cameras come already loaded with film.

Lenses

If you have only one lens for your 35mm camera, chances are that it is a lens between 35mm and 55mm. More photographs have been shot with lenses in this size range than any other, and they are adequate for many uses. The number, which is stamped or painted on the inside rim or outside of the lens, refers to the **focal length** of the lens.

Focal length is measured when the lens is focused at **infinity** (the point at which the farthest objects are in focus). The focal length is the distance from the center of the outside lens element to the point inside the camera where the light rays meet (the point of focus). The focal length number also describes relatively how wide of an area the lens sees. For example, an SLR camera lens with a low focal length number—24mm, 28mm, or 35mm—is usually a wide-angle lens. It takes in a wider view than a 50mm lens. The shorter the focal length, the wider the view.

Wide-angle lenses are especially useful for shooting groups of people and large objects in small spaces. They are also good for shooting landscapes and other scenes where you want to show a large, wide area.

One thing to keep in mind when using wide-angle lenses is that they tend to distort images when they reduce the wide field of view to fit on film. This distortion is most noticeable in photographs of buildings, roadways, and other subjects that involve parallel lines. The shorter the focal length, the greater the distortion.

Telephoto lenses, which generally have an effective focal length of 85mm or longer, have narrower views than standard and wide-angle lenses. While the view is narrower, the image captured on film appears magnified and objects seem closer.

Telephoto lenses are useful when you are shooting a subject from a distance. Long telephoto lenses, ranging from 200mm to 600mm, are especially useful for shooting wildlife and sporting events. Telephoto lenses between 85mm and 105mm are sometimes referred to as portrait lenses. They allow photographers to emphasize their subjects by focusing tightly on their features while blurring the background.

One characteristic of telephoto lenses is that they compress the images within their field of view. Objects in the distance appear much closer together than they really are.

Both the 105mm (3) and 200mm (4) lenses are long-range lenses that bring a portion of the scene in closer.

Zoom lenses are lenses that can be adjusted to different focal lengths. Some common ranges are 80-200mm and 35-135mm. Zoom lenses are versatile, and they can be used in place of several different lenses. Their main drawbacks are that they are longer and bulkier than fixed focal length lenses, and they require more light. On many zoom lenses, the widest aperture is only 4.5.

Focus

To capture sharp images on film, the lens of your camera must be focused. With automatic and fixed-focus cameras, focusing is done for you. With manual cameras, you must focus the lens accurately if you want to record clear, recognizable images.

Manual cameras are focused by turning a ring on the lens. This moves the elements (the pieces of glass that make up the lens) either farther away from or closer to the film plane. When the elements are moved away as far as they will go, subjects close to the lens are in focus. When the elements are moved in as tight as possible, the opposite is true. Distant objects will be sharp, while subjects that are near will be blurred.

Most adjustable-focus cameras have a focusing screen, which is visible through the viewfinder. In many SLR cameras, there are two small half circles visible in the middle of the viewfinder. When the lens is focused accurately, the two halves match at the center, and the image is sharp. When unfocused, the two images split apart.

Most **range-finder** cameras have a viewfinder that is separate from the lens. Unfocused images appear in the viewfinder as double images. When the double images are matched into one, the camera is focused.

Always focus on the subject you want to emphasize. If you are focusing on people or animals, focus on their eyes. This will ensure that the rest of their facial features will be reasonably sharp.

Zoom lenses can help you to capture razor sharp images. After you have framed your subject, zoom in by moving the lens to its longest focal length. Focus on the texture of the building, or the weave of your subject's sweater. If you're shooting a person or an animal, focus on the eyes or hair. Then adjust the focal length back to include the entire scene you wish to record, and shoot. The focus will stay the same.

Automatic Focusing Systems

Many modern cameras, primarily point-and-shoot models and SLR models, come with an automatic focusing system that takes care of the focusing for you. Some cameras, usually point-and-shoot cameras, use a system that bounces a beam of infrared light off the subject and sets the focus for the distance the beam travels. Other cameras, usually SLRs, scan the image as it appears in the lens and focus until an acceptable level of sharpness is reached.

If you use an auto-focus camera, read the manual carefully to determine the best way to use the feature.

Many cameras set the focus on whatever is in the center of the shot. If your main subject is off to one side, you may have to use special techniques to ensure that the shot is in focus.

Most automatic-focus cameras are able to focus on a subject more accurately than the human eye can. However, a photographer has the ability to adjust the focus for special circumstances—to achieve maximum depth of field, for example. Similarly, auto-focus cameras often cannot keep up with the fast action of some subjects, such as bicycle riders.

The *top* photo, shot at f-16, is fairly sharp throughout. In the *bottom* photo, shot at f-2.8, only the front person is in focus. Depth of field is greater at smaller apertures, such as f-16, than at larger apertures, such as f-2.8.

Depth of Field

How can you be sure how much of a scene will be in focus? By using a depth-of-field scale. This scale is located on many of the interchangeable lenses used with 35mm cameras.

Depth of field is the depth—or distance—of focus within the field in view. It indicates how much of a scene is in acceptable focus.

There is a direct relationship between the aperture of a lens and depth of field. The smaller the aperture, the greater the depth of field, or area in focus. Remember, however, there is also a direct relationship between aperture and shutter speed. When you decrease the amount of light reaching the lens, you must increase the length of time the shutter stays open.

Film

The most important step in taking good pictures is loading the film properly. Some cameras use 110 film cassettes, which drop into place. Some 35mm cameras load the film automatically once the cassette is inserted and the leader is situated properly. Other 35mm cameras must be loaded manually.

Some cameras "read" the film speed and automatically set the camera for it. Other cameras must be adjusted by hand. The speed of a film indicates how sensitive it is to light. An international scale, known as ISO, is used to measure and rate film speeds. This scale is also commonly called by its old name, ASA.

You should consider film speed and choose the correct film for different uses. Slower films, such as ISO 25, need much more light than faster, more sensitive films. Slower films can record small details because the grains that make up the images are small and tightly packed. Negatives from these slower films can be enlarged many times without distortion.

You can use fast films, like ISO 1000 or 3200, in dim light. However, the grains of faster films are larger. If the image is enlarged, the print may appear gritty. An ISO of 100 is common for many kinds of color films. In black-and-white film, an ISO of 400 is popular.

Three basic types of film are commonly used: black-and-white film, color print film, and color slide film. Slide film produces color positives, or **transparencies**, that can be projected onto a screen or made into prints. Color and black-and-white print film

A tripod will help keep the camera steady when you are shooting at slow shutter speeds or when you are using long, heavy lenses.

produces **negatives**, which are made into prints to produce positive images.

Tripods

A tripod is a portable, three-legged stand to which you can attach a camera. Use a tripod to keep your camera steady when shooting with a normal lens at shutter speeds of 60 or slower. If you are using a lens of 135mm or longer, use a tripod at speeds slower than 125.

As you increase the size or focal length of your lens, you may have a difficult time trying to keep the camera steady by hand. A good rule of thumb is to increase your shutter speed as you increase the size of your lens. For example, if you are using a 200mm lens, you should use a tripod to support the camera if you use a shutter speed slower than 250.

Camera Bags

A padded camera bag can help protect your equipment and make it easier to carry. Many camera bags have extra pockets to hold film and lenses and have padded carrying straps. Be sure to choose one that is big enough to hold the equipment you have now, with extra room to hold any equipment you might get later.

Nearly all camera equipment is delicate. You should store your equipment in a camera bag that has padded sides and padded inserts to protect the camera body, lenses, filters, and electronic flash from damage.

Light Meters

Most 35mm cameras have built-in **light meters** that either set or recommend the proper exposure. In many adjustable cameras, the exposure setting—a combination of aperture and shutter speed—is displayed in the viewfinder. Many of these cameras use a needle to indicate the proper exposure. When the needle is in the center of the brackets, the exposure is correct. If the needle points up, the image will end up overexposed, or washed out. If the needle points down, the exposure is too low. Details will disappear when the image is too light or too dark.

Filters

UV filters are used more often than any other kind of filter. These clear-looking filters absorb ultraviolet (UV) radiation, which can appear as haze on photographs. Photographers frequently use UV filters to protect camera lenses from dust, scratches, and sometimes even breakage.

Polarizing filters are also popular with photographers. In addition to reducing glare, polarizing filters can accentuate clouds, cut down on reflections, and bring out the blue color in the sky. The photograph *above* was enhanced with a polarizing filter. Without it, the sky and clouds might have blended together too much. When shooting black-and-white film, you can use a red or yellow filter to darken clouds.

Other types of filters soften images, create special effects, or allow you to use normal daylight film indoors under tungsten lights (lights that cast a yellowish tint).

In addition to compensating for certain conditions, filters can protect your lenses from damage and dust. If you were to drop the camera, a filter might absorb the impact and break instead of the lens. Filters are much less expensive to replace than lenses.

Motor Drives

Motor drives, or power winders, advance film automatically and rapidly after you push the shutter button. They are especially useful for shooting the fast action of sports, or for any other situation in which your subject is moving quickly.

Chapter Three

COMPOSITION: CREATING GOOD PICTURES

By incorporating repeated patterns and shapes, such as columns, as well as textures, such as the thistles on a plant, you can create photographic images that stand out.

Taking interesting photographs is easy if you remember the basic elements of photographic composition, or placement. When taking a picture, you, the photographer, are in charge. You make all the decisions!

Everyone has his or her own opinions as to what makes a good photograph. By including one or more of the basic elements in your photographs, you can improve your chances of capturing images that will appeal to a wide variety of people.

You can use the **rule of thirds** to balance your photographs and draw attention to the main subject. Your viewpoint, where you choose to place the camera in relation to your subject, affects the composition. It also sets a mood and establishes a sense of scale.

By identifying and using repeated shapes, patterns, and textures, you can produce dynamic and striking photographs. You can use lines to show perspective and depth, and use foreground framing to enhance a subject. Look for contrasting, or opposite, elements to help your subject stand out.

There are no hard and fast rules in photography. In fact, some of the best images are created by photographers who break the rules. But the basic elements, used by photographers worldwide, can help you produce successful photographs. By keeping these elements in mind, and by learning to see how the camera sees, you will be able to use your camera as a tool to present your view of the world.

Learning to See How the Camera Sees

Learning to see how the camera sees is the most important lesson you can master if you want to take good photographs. When you look around a room, your eyes see selectively —they see what they want to see. They focus on a person or an object, and they tend to ignore the rest of the scene. The camera, however, does not discriminate. It sees everything in its range.

You can look through a camera, for example, and see just your brother. The camera "sees" him, as well as the couch he is sitting on, the picture on the wall behind him, and the lamp to his left. By concentrating on seeing everything the viewfinder sees— by learning to see photographically—you can decide what you want to include or exclude in your photographs.

Looking at things photographically is easy, but it takes practice. Every time you pick up a camera, concentrate on seeing everything in the viewfinder. You can also practice this without a camera. If you get into the habit of seeing photographically, you will find yourself taking more photographs and fewer snapshots.

Seeing photographically will enable you to plan your shots. It will also help you to avoid most of the common mistakes that beginning photographers make. One of the most common mistakes is ignoring the background and taking a picture of a person in front of a tree or plant. In the photograph the tree will look like it is growing out of your subject's head.

Another common mistake is taking a photograph that is too "busy," one that has too many elements in it, all competing for attention. Watch out for backgrounds that are cluttered. Telephone wires, for example, can spoil a scenic or nature shot.

Don't be afraid, however, to experiment. Sometimes, by breaking the rules, you can come up with unusual and dramatic photos. Don't be afraid to make mistakes. That's how you learn.

Choosing Your Subject

One of the first decisions that you, as a photographer, will have to make is about your subject. Who or what do you want to photograph? Your choice is endless. Very often, ordinary, everyday subjects can produce extraordinary, one-of-a-kind photographs.

Once you have decided what to photograph, you must then decide what you want to say about your subject. One question you might want to ask yourself is, What attracted me to this subject in the first place? If your subject is a friend, was it her smile, the goofy hat he was wearing, or just the fact that it is your friend? Once you have answered this question, then ask yourself, What do I want to highlight in my photograph? Often it will be the

A cluttered background will compete with your subject for the viewer's attention.

Emphasize your subject by moving him away from objects that fall into your depth of field and by moving closer so his head and hat fill the viewfinder.

same thing that caught your attention to begin with.

After you have chosen your subject, you must decide how to emphasize it in your photograph. Suppose you decide to take a picture of your friend because the goofy hat he has on makes you laugh. Your friend becomes your subject. His hat is the feature you want to emphasize. The mood you want to capture is laughter.

One way to emphasize the hat is by moving closer to your friend so his head and hat fill the viewfinder frame. This way the background will not compete for attention with the hat. Another way to emphasize the hat is by stepping back and including something in the foreground, like the handrail of the porch stairs between your friend and the camera in order to draw the viewer's eyes to your friend's head.

Balance and Imbalance— The Rule of Thirds

Another way to highlight your subject is to use the rule of thirds. Photographers and artists have discovered that placing or positioning a subject off-center helps it to stand out in the finished photograph. The easiest way to do this is to use the rule of thirds.

Imagine that your viewfinder has four lines drawn on it: two going from right to left above

Oftentimes, by placing your subject along one of the grid lines, or where two grid lines intersect, you can create a dynamic, well-composed image.

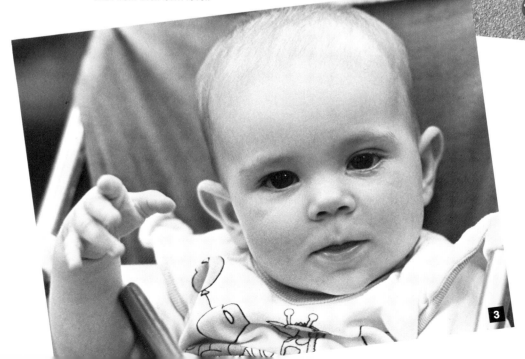

Crouching down and shooting up at your subject (1) makes her appear to tower above the camera. Standing above your subject and shooting down at her (2) has the opposite effect. It dwarfs your subject and makes her appear smaller and weaker. Babies and small children (3) are best captured on film when shot from their own level.

Shooting from different viewpoints can lend a different mood to a photograph and make it visually exciting.

and below the center, and two going up and down to the left and right of the center. Each pair of lines divides the frame into three equal parts. Placing a subject along any of the lines, or at the point where any two lines intersect, will produce a photograph that is interesting and appealing. Generally, photographs that have the main subject centered in the middle of the frame look stiff and unnatural.

Landscapes produce pleasingly balanced photographs if the rule of thirds is employed. Keeping the sky, for example, confined to the upper third of the frame emphasizes the scenery.

Viewpoint

Viewpoint refers to the position of your camera in relation to your subject. Each subject can be shot from hundreds of different viewpoints. Before you take your next picture, experiment with various possibilities. Move around your subject and look at it through the viewfinder from several different angles, up or down, right or left. Unless you are shooting a stationary object, like a house or a tree, you can also have your subject move. Don't be afraid to take your time. Explore all the possibilities before you decide which angle or viewpoint will work best for you.

Your choice of viewpoint will also emphasize the size of your subjects and will convey a mood. Standing above your subjects and shooting down will make them look smaller and weaker. Crouching down and shooting up will make your subjects appear bigger and more powerful.

Some subjects, like children and pets, are best captured if you crouch down and shoot from their level. One of the easiest ways to experiment with viewpoints is to turn your camera vertically. Instead of a horizontal photograph, you will get a vertical one. This is useful if you want to fill the frame and your subject is taller than it is wide.

Repeating Patterns and Shapes

Photographs of repeating patterns or shapes, such as the lines of hills in a landscape, convey a feeling of harmony and order.

You can capture a similar mood by photographing an orderly row of sailboats. Photographs that repeat the same patterns and shapes usually produce soothing images.

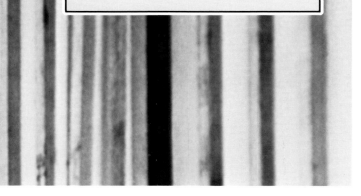

This carpenter stands out because his body contrasts sharply with the repetitive lines of the building.

Contrasting Elements

Patterns can also be used to produce **contrast** and to emphasize a subject. Any time you show the unexpected, or something that is different from the background, you are using contrast to highlight your subject. If your subject breaks the pattern, it will attract attention.

Using color to emphasize contrast produces striking results. A yellow block in a stack of blue blocks leaps out at the viewer. So does the child who steps out of a line. Contrasting your subject with larger or smaller elements is another technique that helps it stand out. A small child standing with a group of basketball players emphasizes both how tall the players are and how small the child is. This technique is often used to illustrate the size of an object. In many scientific photographs, for example, a coin or other familiar object is placed next to the specimen to lend a sense of scale.

Textures

Although photography is something that appeals to your sense of sight, you can use it to appeal to your sense of touch as well. A crisply focused photograph of a coil of rope emphasizes the rough texture of the fibers. Texture also conveys the subject's depth or bulk.

Use of Lines

Lines in your photographs can add a sense of depth, and they can also illustrate moods. In addition, lines tend to draw a viewer's eyes from one subject to another by forming a visual connection between the elements.

Curving lines that connect subjects soften the mood of a photograph and make it appear more graceful. Diagonal lines, going from an upper corner to the opposite lower corner, create an impression of restlessness. Horizontal lines, from left to right, suggest a sense of balance and calm. Vertical lines illustrate height and a sense of grandeur.

Parallel lines, like those of a train track, appear to move closer together as they disappear toward the horizon. Parallel lines are often used to successfully illustrate distance or depth.

Putting It All Together

Learn how to see photographically. Before you take a picture, visualize how the finished photograph will look. Examine the background closely.

After you have chosen your subject, ask yourself what attracted you to it. This will help you decide which features to emphasize.

Before you shoot, ask yourself these questions: Will this picture be enhanced by using the rule of thirds? What viewpoint should I shoot from? Is there a repeating pattern or shape I want to emphasize? Is there a contrasting element that will help to highlight my subject? Can I use texture or lines to illustrate depth?

Don't be afraid to experiment. Remember, ordinary subjects can make extraordinary photographs.

Foreground Framing

You can enhance pictures, including informal portraits, by positioning your subject within a natural frame, like the open top half of a Dutch door.

A frame around a photograph or a painting highlights it by drawing the viewer's eyes to what is inside the frame. Parts of your photograph can do the same thing to your main subject if they frame it. A natural frame, such as the arch of a bridge, makes a photograph of a stream more interesting by adding perspective. Two trees, bending and touching at the top, also make a good frame for a photograph of joggers running underneath. Look around for natural frames that can enhance your composition. If your subject is a person, don't be afraid to ask him or her to move if another position will work better for you.

Chapter Four

PHOTOGRAPHY AND LIGHT

Light is essential to photography, and many photographers emphasize its dramatic effects. However, you can have too much light. *Opposite*, direct sunlight usually causes your subjects to squint and creates harsh shadows on their faces.

Light is essential to photography. In fact, the word photography comes from two Greek words that together mean "to draw by light." Light allows your eyes and the lens of your camera to see. Light rays that reflect off a subject and into your camera lens are what expose your film when you press the shutter button.

Natural Light

There are two basic sources of light— natural light from the sun and the moon, and artificial or manufactured light. Natural light, which is sometimes referred to as available light, is constantly changing. Not only does it change throughout the day as the sun moves across the sky, but it also changes with the seasons and with the weather.

The changes in light make a difference in the way your photographs look. The amount of light available, and the angle at which it strikes your subject, affects the tones of your photographs, as well as the brightness of the colors. Light can help create the mood of a photograph.

Although light is necessary for photography, it is possible to have too much of a good thing. Bright, sunny days are good for shooting landscapes and sports events. Too much sunshine, however, can sometimes cause problems for photographers. Bright light, which is strongest between 10 A.M. and 2 P.M., produces strong contrasts and can make your subjects squint and look harsh. Bright light also casts dark shadows that can hide details. Bright light can also make the colors in your photographs look faded and washed out.

You can still get great photographs in bright daylight. You can move your subject into the shade, where the light is softer. If you do, be sure to take your light-meter reading close to your subject. That way, the reading

The softer light in the shade on a bright day is usually better than direct sunlight. Check the background for bright light that might cause your light meter to misread the correct exposure.

won't be influenced by the dark shadows, or by the bright sunlight.

If your subject is stationary, walk around it and see if there is a better angle from which to shoot. You can also wait for the sun to hide behind a cloud, or you could come back later in the day when the light is softer.

Early morning and late afternoon, when the sun is low on the horizon, can be good times to take pictures. When the light strikes the Earth at a low angle, it is softer, or muted. Colors take on darker and deeper hues, and there is less contrast. Shadows may be longer, but they are softer. Sunrise and sunset are good times to take photographs too. The dramatic red hues produced at these times of day can turn ordinary subjects into extraordinarily beautiful photographs.

Experiment with different angles, or different light conditions. One of the best ways to learn about light is to choose a stationary subject and take pictures of it at different times of the day or even different times of the year. To see what settings produce the best results, **bracket** your exposures by shooting photographs at the recommended exposure, as well as at f-stops above and below the recommended exposure. With practice, you can learn how to take good pictures in many different kinds of light.

Artificial Light

You can also take pictures indoors under artificial light. Because the light from lamps and light bulbs is not as bright as the sun, you may have to use a faster film, with an ISO of 400 or more, and use a slower shutter speed along with a wide aperture setting.

Don't be afraid to move your light sources, or to ask your subject to move closer to the light. Flash attachments also provide additional illumination.

Light changes throughout the day and creates different effects. This scene, shot in the morning (1), at noon (2), and in the evening (3), shows the differences.

When available lighting is dim or unevenly spread across your subject, supplement it with an electronic flash.

Depending on the type of artificial light (incandescent, tungsten, or florescent), you will see red, yellow, or blue hues in your color photographs. To combat this, use special film that is made for indoor light.

The Direction of Light: Front, Back, and Side Lighting

The direction of your light source is also important. Front lighting, where the sun or other light source is shining directly on your subject, can make your subject look harsh. It can also flatten any textures in your photograph.

Side lighting creates the opposite effect. It can give dimension and form to your subjects and bring out textures. It sometimes creates unusual shadows.

Back lighting, where the light source is directly behind your subject, can be the most difficult lighting to use effectively. When using back lighting, you must take your light-meter reading close to the subject. That way, your camera won't be influenced by the bright light coming from behind and won't underexpose the subject.

Back lighting can be used to create some interesting effects, especially if the light shines directly through an object, like the leaves of a tree or the windows of a building. It can also be used to create dramatic silhouettes. The trick to shooting silhouettes is to first take a light-meter reading of your subject, then underexpose the film by two f-stops.

Experiment with the light coming from different directions. Ask a friend to pose for you, or use a stationary object.

Flash

Electronic flash units are easy to use, and they are a great way to provide indoor and outdoor illumination at night. You might also find yourself using a flash outdoors during the daytime as "fill-in" light to eliminate shadows. Most electronic flashes attach to the hot shoe of your camera. Some must also be plugged into the front of the camera. When you press the shutter, the flash unit will provide a quick, intense flash of light.

When using a flash, you must set the shutter speed of most cameras at 60 or slower. If you set the shutter speed faster than the camera's **sync speed**, or the setting at which the shutter and flash are synchronized, you will very likely underexpose a large strip of your picture. Check the manual that came with your camera for the correct shutter speed setting. On many cameras, the recommended setting is indicated on the shutter ring by an X next to the shutter speed number.

Making the Most Out of Bad Weather

Foggy, rainy, and overcast days can be good times to take pictures. These conditions diffuse, or soften, sunlight. This soft, even light eliminates shadows that can hide details. Bad weather can sometimes produce interesting clouds as well.

Dark, rainy days can also create a special mood in photographs. Be careful, however, to keep your camera dry. Stand under a ledge or protect your camera in a plastic bag. You can use a rubber band to secure the opening of the bag around your lens.

Getting good pictures of people on the move requires some special techniques, as well as good timing.

Chapter Five

CAPTURING THE ACTION

Fast shutter speeds, such as 500, 1000, and even 2000 and 4000, allow modern cameras to freeze action. Fast shutter speeds are especially useful for shooting sporting events, moving vehicles, and anything else that is moving quickly.

A little planning can go a long way toward capturing exciting action shots. It's hard to focus on a moving subject, especially one that is moving rapidly. Position yourself ahead of the action and preset your exposure (f-stop and shutter speed) and focus. You can focus on one of the bases on a baseball field, for example, or the edge of a racetrack. When your subject moves into your area of focus, just press the shutter button.

Motor drives are especially useful for sports photography. If you shoot three or four frames as your subject moves within your field of view, you will increase your odds of capturing a sharp image.

Panning

Another way to capture the action on film and to convey a sense of movement is to pan your camera while you shoot. Preset your exposure and focus, using a shutter speed of 60 or slower. Aim your camera at your subject and follow it with the lens as it goes past. Press the shutter when the subject is directly in front of you, and keep panning, or following through, on your shot. The result is a blurred or streaked background, which conveys a sense of speed.

Anticipating the Action

Often the best sports photos are taken by photographers who know the sport they are shooting well. Try taking pictures of your friends playing your favorite sport. Use your familiarity with the game to plan ahead and anticipate the action.

Some photographers like to position themselves so they can capture the scoring. At a basketball game, they stand near the hoop. Others prefer to move along the sidelines and shoot from various angles.

If you are shooting a sport that is unfamiliar to you, take some time to figure out where most of the action takes place. Then position yourself and your camera accordingly. Whichever sport or position you choose is up to you. Just remember to stay clear of the action.

Chapter Six

PORTRAITS

One of the most difficult tasks for photographers is trying to obtain portraits that show their subjects' personalities. *Far left:* Some of the best portraits are taken when subjects are unaware of the camera. *Left:* Children can be easier to photograph if you distract them with toys or other objects.

For many photographers, families and friends are favorite subjects. Why? Good photographs of people can provide great memories, especially if they capture the character and personality of their subjects. The better you know a person, the easier it will be for you to capture his or her spirit along with the photographic image.

Adults

Many adults are self-conscious in front of a camera. One way to get them to relax is to make them forget you are taking their picture. Shoot photographs of people when they are active, especially if they are doing something they really enjoy.

If there is nothing to distract your subject, you can often get them to relax by talking and

joking with them. Take several frames so you can choose the pose you like best.

Children

Young children are usually much more relaxed in front of a camera. When photographing young children, however, you have to work fast. They generally have short attention spans and can move quite quickly. If possible, use a medium-fast shutter speed (at least 250) to freeze the action. If you give your young subjects something to play with, you can sometimes occupy them long enough to take their pictures.

Try to shoot pictures of children in bright light. This allows you to use a small aperture and a rapid shutter speed, which will increase your depth of field and ensure that your young subjects remain in focus even if they move a little closer to or farther away from your lens.

When shooting young children, kneel or squat down to their level. Standing upright and shooting down at small subjects will make their heads appear large and their bodies seem small and frail.

Formal Portraits

Many portrait photographers prefer to use a medium telephoto lens, between 75mm and 135mm, to shoot portraits. Longer focal length lenses allow you to keep a comfortable distance from your subjects, while still allowing them to fill the frame. These lenses also allow you to focus tightly on facial features, which will help blur out the background. A larger aperture setting, like f-2.8 or f-4, will also help minimize the background by shortening the depth of field.

When shooting formal portraits, position your subjects to obtain ideal lighting. Avoid bright overhead light when possible. Like sunlight, it creates harsh shadows on the subjects' faces.

To make the best use of available light, you can place your subjects alongside a light-colored wall, which will

Placing your subjects in some sort of context, such as their jobs or a leisure activity, makes your portraits more interesting.

reflect light onto them. You can also use handmade reflectors. Cover a piece of flat cardboard with crumpled aluminum foil, and use it to reflect light onto your subject.

If you have a manual camera, take your light-meter reading off the face, then add one stop to the reading. Shoot several frames so you can choose the pose you like best.

Informal Portraits

Candid photographs and informal portraits often reveal more of a subject's personality than formal portraits. Capture images of your family and friends engaged in conversation or absorbed in their favorite activities. A medium-long telephoto lens will allow you to maintain a good distance. With a 75mm or 135mm lens, you can sometimes take pictures without your subject's knowledge.

Environmental Photographs

Pictures of people in their own environment—at home, at work, or at play—can be very revealing. The background can help tell the story. A photograph of a nurse in uniform and working in a hospital can say more about that person than a picture of the same person posing outside in street clothes.

A teacher at a blackboard, a firefighter at the scene of a fire, and a police officer directing traffic make interesting subjects for environmental portraits. Ask your parents and older siblings if you can photograph them at their jobs.

Chapter Seven

PHOTOGRAPHING ANIMALS

You can get good photographs of animals in a zoo, *far left*, where these flamingos live, or in their natural habitat, *above*, such as the beach where this sea lion chose to warm itself.

Animals are another favorite subject of photographers. Whether it is the family dog dozing in the sun, a hummingbird in flight, or a pride of lions racing across an African plain, animals are fascinating and can make interesting photographs.

Animals in the Wild

You don't have to go on a camera safari to Kenya to take pictures of wild animals in their home environments. Wild animals are all around, whether you live in a city, a suburb, or in a rural area. You can spot birds, squirrels, chipmunks, raccoons, possums, skunks, or even a deer or two in your area.

Even if you live in an apartment building, you can usually attract wildlife to your window or balcony by installing a bird or squirrel feeder. Be patient, however. It usually takes a week or more before animals will come to a new feeder.

43

Another option is to go where the animals are. Lakes, ponds, streams, and other bodies of water often attract many animals. You can also visit parks, nature preserves, and wildlife sanctuaries. The local guides and rangers can usually provide you with information about the animals that inhabit the area.

An understanding of an animal's habits, as well as patience, can help you to obtain great nature photographs. Some animals, for example, seek food and water mainly at dawn and dusk. If you wait patiently at one of their favorite water holes during those times, you'll have a better chance of capturing rewarding images.

A telephoto lens between 135mm and 400mm can be helpful. A long lens will usually allow you to take pictures without frightening or disturbing your subjects. The longer the telephoto lens, however, the more difficult it will be to focus.

Below: a squirrel in the park is a not-so-obvious choice for a photograph. *Above right:* while many zoo animals are confined in enclosures that allow you to photograph them in a natural-looking environment, including the bars of a cage can sometimes enhance the photograph.

Zoo Animals

Zoos are great places to photograph animals. Many zoos now keep their animals in barrier-free enclosures, rather than behind bars. Photographers have never had an easier time getting natural-looking shots of captive animals.

Even behind bars, zoo animals can make good subjects. You can use the bars to frame and enhance your subject, or you can blur them out of focus. A wide aperture, like f-2.8, will result in a shallow depth of field. By focusing on the animal's eyes, you can capture a sharp image of your subject, while the bars of the cage almost disappear.

Resist the temptation to race around and snap pictures of as many different zoo animals as you can. Instead, spend time watching the animals you find especially interesting. If you are patient, you will increase your chances of getting a really good shot.

Pets

Family pets also make great subjects. Cats and dogs can be active, however, and difficult to photograph unless you catch them during a calm moment. Wait until your cat relaxes in a sunbeam, or after a meal. With dogs, you will have an easier time taking their picture after exercising them, not before. Squat or kneel down, and shoot from their level for a distortion-free image.

Pets are often easier to photograph if they're occupied. Have a friend or family member play with your subject. This will keep your pet from scampering away or walking up to you and nuzzling your lens.

A relatively fast shutter speed, 250 or greater, will generally freeze a squirming pet. Use fast film, ISO 200 or faster, or shoot in bright light so you can stop down your aperture and increase your depth of field. A larger area of focus increases your chances of capturing a sharp image of a moving pet.

Pets make great subjects, if you can get them to remain still long enough to take their picture. Like young children, cats and dogs are easier to photograph if they are distracted.

Chapter Eight

LANDSCAPES AND CITYSCAPES

A great landscape photograph is like a good portrait. It captures the essence and spirit of an area.

Few photographers can resist the urge to record scenic images, such as landscapes and cityscapes. The views created by nature and by humans can make fascinating subjects.

Landscapes

A good landscape photograph not only records the scenery and produces a souvenir of a family vacation or class field trip, but it also captures the character of the scene.

Landscapes, as well as other scenes shot at infinity, illustrate the ability of camera lenses to capture, precisely, a large area. Miles and miles of scenery can be captured on a 35mm negative, which is about 1 inch by 1½ inches (about 25mm by 35mm) in size. Because so

many images are condensed and recorded, it is important to isolate your main subject. Ask yourself, what sights made me decide to photograph this scene?

The main subject of your shot might be the sweeping curve of a bay, a chain of snow-capped mountains, or the vibrant colors of a meadow full of wildflowers.

Once you have isolated your viewpoint, take time to compose your shot. If you use one or more of the elements of composition, you will increase your chances of producing clear and interesting landscape pictures.

Including any easily recognizable objects in the foreground, such as animals, people, or trees, will help give your photographs a sense of depth and provide a size reference.

Above: The vivid colors of these wildflowers create an exciting image. *Opposite:* Cityscape photographs can include old buildings contrasted against modern buildings and natural images contrasted against manufactured images, as well as skylines and other popular city images.

Experiment with different viewpoints and observe the light at different times during the day. Early morning and late afternoon are often the best times to shoot scenery. The low angle of the sun helps to accentuate shapes and other features in the landscape. Bright midday sun often casts shadows that can hide details. Sometimes, however, that same harsh sunlight creates interesting patterns.

Changes in the weather and the seasons also affect the way a scene looks. Dark storm clouds add a dramatic look to a landscape. If that's the case, you might want to include a good portion of the sky in your shot. A polarizing filter can help cut the glare and make the clouds look more dramatic.

Lakes, ponds, puddles, and other bodies of water generally reflect images and light. The effect is so appealing that many photographers choose to include them in landscape photos whenever possible. However, while a polarizing filter can help cut down on the glare of reflected light, it will also lessen reflections that you might want to emphasize.

A small aperture will ensure that most or all of the scene will be in focus. If you are using a manual camera, take your exposure reading on the main subject of your scene, and exclude the sky. Shoot several frames and bracket your exposures to increase your chances of capturing a properly exposed photograph.

Landscapes aren't limited to panoramas, or large unobstructed views of a scene. Sometimes a closer view is preferred. A single tree, a leaf, a stream, a sand dune, or a strand of moss dangling from a branch are just a few interesting subjects you might find in the landscape. You can isolate specific subjects by using a large aperture to create a shallow depth of field. Then focus tightly on your subject to make it stand out from the unfocused background.

Cityscapes

All of the same techniques used for capturing clear and interesting landscapes can be applied to shooting cityscapes. Isolate your main subject, and explore all the possible viewpoints—including looking up, which will exaggerate height.

Look for patterns, like a row of matching houses, shadows, unusual shapes, or interesting details. Contrasting elements, like an old church surrounded by new buildings, or a small structure surrounded by larger ones, make interesting shots.

Frame your shot to minimize or exclude distracting elements, like moving vehicles, pedestrians, or electrical wires. If the horizon is in your field of view, make sure it is straight in your viewfinder.

As with shooting landscapes, a small aperture will ensure that a greater area is in focus. The same exposure rules apply as well. Take your readings off the subject, not off the sky, and bracket your exposure.

Chapter Nine

COLOR

Color can greatly enhance photographs. The yellow jackets worn by firefighters (1) stand out against the softer colors of the house. A photograph of kids and balloons (2) would not be the same without bright colors. Nature (3) is full of all shades of colors.

Color adds yet another dimension to photography. Many photographers take color for granted because color film is relatively inexpensive. They ignore the fact that careful use of color can greatly enhance a photograph.

Learn to look for color and use it to your advantage when you compose your shots. As well as adding to the visual impact, color helps capture the mood. Bright, vibrant yellows add excitement to a photograph, while fiery reds and oranges convey warmth. Blues and greens create a cool, yet soothing, effect.

3

Bright colors stand out even more if they are contrasted against different colored backgrounds. A bright red balloon stands out against the blue sky. During a sunrise or sunset that has bathed the sky in red and orange, however, that same red balloon won't look as brilliant.

When composing for color, don't ignore the beauty of softer colors. Soft, pastel colors, like a field of wildflowers in a green meadow, can also produce stunning photographs. Soft, subtle colors also make good backgrounds for brightly colored objects.

A child in a bright yellow raincoat, for example, really stands out against a gray building.

Color in photography is created by light. Like light, color changes throughout the day and with the seasons. The colors of a scene will be different in photos shot at different times of the day or at different times of the year. Bright light enhances bright colors, although extremely bright light and glare will wash out the colors. Early morning and late evening light bathes everything in warm, reddish tones.

The bright colors on this train, *right,* stand out in contrast to the subdued colors elsewhere to produce a vibrant photograph. Color contrast is less evident, but the evening sky, *below,* produces a dramatic photograph with its soothing colors.

‿‿‿‿ Lighting for Color ‿‿‿‿

Bright light emphasizes brilliant colors, although the shadows it casts will usually hide the details of darker colors. In this photograph, the sunlight, coming from the right, brings out the yellow of the wild mustard flowers and allows them to contrast sharply with the green grass and stems. The darkest objects in the photograph, such as the tree branches and the bushes, lose details.

Softer light, such as the diffused light of overcast days,

will make colors softer and less brilliant. However, your photographs are more apt to convey a dramatic mood. While diffused lighting frequently lacks the ability to bring out contrast, it can add details, such as texture, to a photograph.

Many professional photographers advise that a photograph should have one dominant subject and a balance between bright colors and softer shades.

Many people prefer black-and-white photography because it is easier to experiment with and because it can highlight content and composition without those elements having to compete with color for the viewer's attention.

Chapter Ten

BLACK AND WHITE

Black-and-white photography can be an excellent medium for beginning photographers, especially those who have access to a school, club, or home darkroom. Many experienced photographers prefer to work in black and white because they can use the special qualities of black-and-white film to their advantage.

Black-and-white film records a scene in shades of gray instead of in color. Some colors, like blue and green, will look the same on a black-and-white print. Learning to visualize a scene in black and white instead of in color may be difficult, but it will help you to make sure your subjects stand out from their backgrounds.

One reason the use of black-and-white film is so popular with young photographers is because it is relatively easy to process and print. Making your own prints allows you to experiment freely with photography. You can shoot many different viewpoints of the same scene, for example, then print only the frames you like best.

Interesting black-and-white photographs often rely on shapes, patterns, and contrasts between dark and light objects. These elements, especially the contrast between light and dark, can set moods or convey feelings. Generally, darker scenes appear somber, or low-key. Lighter scenes can convey an upbeat feel.

Often the impact of a photograph is stronger in black and white because the subject is not competing with color for a viewer's attention.

Chapter Eleven

SPECIAL EFFECTS

If you have a zoom lens, you can create photographs with the special effects shown on these pages.

You can use special effects to create images that are exciting and different. Even if you don't use special effects very often, they can provide some fun experiments.

Zooming for the Effect of Motion

Zoom lenses, combined with a slow shutter speed, can produce interesting results. If you zoom your lens in or out to reduce or increase its focal length while the shutter is open, you can capture images with an unusual motion effect.

The best way to get this effect is to put your camera on a tripod to keep it steady, then zoom in or out while using a shutter speed of 8 or slower.

The light created by fireworks can be captured on film if you use a tripod and a very slow shutter speed.

Time Exposures

Lights at night make fascinating subjects for time exposures. The darkness will require you to use an extremely slow shutter speed. Any movement of light sources, like fireworks or car headlights, will create streaks of light.

Set your camera on a tripod and set your shutter setting on B, or bulb. Use a cable release to hold the camera lens open and let your subjects move past it. The result will be a photograph that shows the path of the lights.

Multiple Exposures

Multiple exposures, where two images are superimposed on a single negative or slide, can be taken with many cameras. Some cameras even have a special control that allows you to shoot as many frames as you wish without advancing the film. Check the manual that came with your camera for specific instructions.

Star Filters

One of the easiest ways to create a special effect is to use a filter designed for that purpose. One such filter is a star filter, which turns points of light into stars of light.

The glints of light reflecting off this hubcap were created with a star filter.

When you set up your darkroom for developing film, you will need the following equipment and chemicals:

roll of exposed film	developing reels	stop bath
can opener	developing tank	fixer
scissors	timer	hypo clearing
lighttight room or	thermometer	agent
changing bag	**developer**	wetting agent

Chapter Twelve

IN THE DARKROOM

Some photographers enjoy working in the darkroom as much as they enjoy taking pictures. Watching a print develop can be exciting, especially if the image is a particularly good one.

Developing and printing your own film gives you another chance to be creative, and offers an opportunity to fine-tune your pictures.

Developing and printing are not difficult to do once someone has shown you how. What follows is basic information about film processing, which will give you an idea of how the process works. You can use this chapter for reference, too.

Developing Black-and-White Film

The basic developing process for black-and-white film is the same no matter which brand of developing chemicals you use. However, the times and temperatures vary with each brand. Always read the instructions that come with your chemicals.

Prepare the chemicals according to the packet instructions. By running hot or cold water on the solution containers, you can adjust the temperatures of the chemicals to within 1 degree of the recommended reading (usually 68 degrees Fahrenheit).

In a completely dark room, open the film cassette with a can opener, cut off the leader, and load the film onto a film reel. Insert the reel into the developing tank and close the lid. Once the lid is properly closed, you can safely turn on a light.

You can also use a changing bag to load the film into the tank. Place the film, can opener, scissors, film reels, tank, and lid into the bag and close it. Insert your arms into the sleeves of the bag and follow the same steps you would use if you were in a lighttight room. Before attempting to load an important roll of film into a developing tank in the dark, you should practice by using a spare roll of film, first in the light, then in the dark.

Once the film has been loaded into a lighttight developing tank, you can turn the lights on and complete the processing.

Once you have loaded your film properly, pour in the developer, seal the second lid, and set the timer. Gently agitate the tank for the first 30 seconds by holding it in your hand and rotating your wrist back and forth. You will also need to agitate the tank every minute the developer is in the tank, for 10 seconds. Pour out the developer at the proper time, then pour in the stop bath solution which stops the developer from acting. After 30 seconds, drain and discard this chemical down the sink drain.

Next, pour in the fixer—which fixes the image on the film and makes it permanent—and agitate the tank for 10 seconds every minute. Drain the fixer when the time is up, disposing of it as directed on the package.

Once the fixer has been drained, you may expose the film to light. Open the lid of the tank and wash the film by placing the tank under a faucet and running water through it. Wash the film for 5 minutes, then add the hypo clearing agent to help get rid of the fixer. Wash the film for an additional 15 minutes. If you're not using a hypo clearing agent, wash the film for 30 minutes.

To prevent water spots from forming on your film as it dries, pour a wetting agent, such as Photoflo, into the developing tank and drain it after 30 seconds. Unroll the film from the reel and hang it up to dry in a dust-free area. Make sure the film does not touch the wall, other rolls of film, or anything else until it is completely dry.

Once the film is dry, cut it into strips of five or six frames and slip them into protective sleeves. You should develop a habit of washing the developing tank, reels, and other equipment after each use to prevent chemical contamination.

Printing Pictures

Once your negatives are dry and have been cut into strips, you are ready to print your photographs. You will need the following equipment and supplies:

four developing trays	developer
safelight	stop bath
enlarger	fixer
timer	resin-coated (RC)
tongs	photographic
printing-paper easel	paper

Set out three of the trays, side by side. Pour developer into the first tray, stop bath into the second one, and fixer into the third one. With the fourth tray, rig up a washing system that allows water to flow in from a faucet, circulate around the tray, and flow out into a sink. Once the trays are in place, you can start making prints.

At the enlarger, with white lights off and the safelight on, project the negative you want to print onto the easel and adjust the focus. Turn off the enlarger and insert a piece of photographic paper into the easel frame. Your exposures will vary with each print, so you will have to experiment with different times and enlarger apertures.

Make test prints by covering all but a fifth of the photographic paper with a piece of cardboard. Expose the uncovered portion for five seconds. Slide the cardboard to uncover another fifth of the photographic paper, then expose the uncovered portions for five seconds. Continue sliding the cardboard over and exposing the print until you have uncovered the entire sheet of paper.

Slip the photographic paper facedown into the tray of developer to ensure that the chemicals reach all parts of the print. Once the paper has been saturated, you can use tongs to flip the paper over and watch the print emerge. Agitate the tray continuously while the print is developing, making sure the paper stays submerged.

Leave the print in the developer for the recommended time, usually about 1 minute. Using tongs, pick up the print by a corner and drain it for 5 to 10 seconds. Then slide the print into the stop bath. After 30 seconds, remove the print, drain off the stop bath solution, and slide the print into the fixer. Leave it in the fixer for 3 to 4 minutes (depending on the type of fixer used) and agitate the tray occasionally. After you take the print out of the fixer, you can turn the light on and evaluate the print. Which time exposure looks best?

Pick the best exposure time and make the whole print at that exposure. Develop your new print just as you developed the test print, but take an additional last step. After removing the print from the fixer, place it in the tray that you set up as a washing system.

Wash the print for 15 minutes with the water running. Drain off the excess water, then use a squeegee along the back (never the front) of the photographic paper to remove the rest of the water. Place the finished print to dry on a drying screen or hang it on a string with clothespins.

Chapter Thirteen

DISPLAYING YOUR WORK

Displaying your photographs, either by framing them, putting on slide shows, or by placing them in photo albums, allows you to share them easily with your family and friends.

Photo Albums

Photo albums are a good way to store and view prints. There are dozens of different photo albums available in stores. Some have plastic sleeves that hold prints and allow you to rearrange photos easily. Others require you to mount your pictures on pages with adhesive-backed photo corners. Most albums can be expanded to hold additional pictures.

Whatever type of photo album or storage system you choose, make sure the holders or pages are "archival." Non-archival pages are made with PVC plastics, which can cause photographs, negatives, and slides to deteriorate over time. If you are buying a scrapbook album, look for one with acid-free pages.

Many photographers save only their best prints and throw the bad ones away after studying their mistakes. If you organize your photo albums by subject or by date, you will have an easier time locating specific pictures.

Framed Prints

You can make enlargements of your favorite pictures (or have them made at a photo lab) and hang them on a wall or display them on a table. Ready-made frames are available at most camera, stationery, and variety stores. These frames are a relatively inexpensive way to display and protect your photographs. You can also purchase precut mats to border your pictures and plastic foam boards to provide a stiff backing for them.

Clip frames, which use plastic or metal clips to hold a piece of glass over a photograph, are another inexpensive way to protect and display your favorite pictures.

Far left: Photo albums give you a place to arrange your photographs and will also protect them from damage. *Left:* Slide projectors are a good way to display your photographs to a group of people at once.

You can also order custom frames from many art stores and framing galleries, but they are more costly than ready-made frames.

Slide Shows

Slide shows are a great way to share your work and the excitement of photography with others. When projected, the images on slides are enlarged considerably. Larger images are generally more lifelike and look more realistic than smaller ones.

Before showing your slides to an audience, sort through them and pick out only your best work. Organize the slides into a sequence that helps to tell a story. A slide show of your sister's softball team, for example, might start with scenes of the team's first practices and end with images taken during or after the final game.

If you don't have a projection screen, you can use a large piece of white cardboard, a white sheet tacked to the wall, or any flat, white wall.

You can still enjoy your slides even if you don't have a projector. You can use an inexpensive slide viewer to look at your slides. Like prints and negatives, slides should be handled with care. Hold them only by their edges.

You can also store and view your slides in protective slide holders. Most brands hold 20 slides on a sheet, which fits neatly into a three-ring binder. These sheets allow you to view the slides while keeping them clean and free of dust.

Studio photographers use a variety of special equipment to control all aspects of their shots.

Chapter Fourteen

CAREERS IN PHOTOGRAPHY

You can display and improve your photography skills now by volunteering to take pictures for your school newspaper or yearbook.

Taking pictures can be more than just a rewarding and entertaining hobby. Some people become professional photographers and earn a living taking pictures. Many others use photography in their jobs.

While You're Still in School

If your school publishes a yearbook or newspaper, volunteer to be one of the photographers. You will gain valuable experience by taking pictures for school publications. Occasionally, community newspapers will hire high school students to take pictures of in-school events, like pep rallies, or after-school events, like concerts. You can also use your camera to illustrate reports and papers you write for class assignments.

Professional Careers

There are many different ways to make a living as a photographer. Some commercial photographers work mainly inside a studio. Many of these photographers specialize in taking portraits, such as engagement pictures and pictures of students. Other commercial photographers use their equipment and photographic knowledge to shoot photographs at weddings and other special events.

Some photographers specialize in taking pictures for advertisements. Advertising photographers work both inside and outside the studio, and they often rely on a wide range of special effects. Still other photographers work as free-lancers, taking on various assignments from anyone who needs special photographs for a particular project.

Photojournalists must be ready to take good photographs under any circumstances.

Photojournalists are photographers who take pictures for newspapers and magazines. Photojournalists usually work quickly to take pictures of events as they are happening. They generally have little control over the circumstances under which they shoot their pictures, so they must be adaptable.

Some photographers specialize in taking pictures in hospitals to help doctors and nurses document medical conditions.

Fine-art photographers take pictures of whatever subjects interest them. These photographs are displayed in galleries, published in books, and sold to people who display them in their homes and offices.

Other photographers make their livings shooting fashion pictures, taking aerial views, or recording events for the military.

Whether you decide to pursue a career as a photographer, or you simply continue to photograph the world around you as a hobby, photography becomes more enjoyable as you try different techniques and see improvement in your skills.

aperture: the adjustable opening in a camera lens that allows light to reach the film. Apertures vary in size and are identified by f-stop numbers.

bracket: to expose the film at f-stops or shutter speeds just above and below the light meter's recommended setting

contrast: the difference between elements in a photograph. Contrast can be the disruption of an orderly arrangement in the composition, the difference between light and dark areas, or a marked difference in colors.

depth of field: the range of distance that is acceptably sharp within a photograph

developer: a chemical solution that changes invisible images exposed on light-sensitive film or paper into a visible image

diaphragm: an adjustable device, usually made of overlapping metal plates, that controls the size of the aperture

enlarger: an essential piece of darkroom equipment that projects an image, usually from a negative, onto an easel. Light-sensitive paper placed on the easel records the projected image.

exposure: the amount of light that reaches film or light-sensitive paper through a combination of aperture size and shutter speed

f-stop: the number assigned to a particular aperture size

fixer: a chemical solution that makes film or photographic paper no longer sensitive to light

focal length: the distance from the optical center of a lens to the focus when the lens is focused at the infinity position

focus: to adjust the distance between the lens and an image to make the image as sharp as possi-ble; also, the point at which parallel light rays meet after passing through a lens

hypo clearing agent: a chemical solution used in developing film and photographic paper as a washing agent and to prolong the life of the image

infinity: the point on the focusing ring at which the farthest object in the lens range is in focus

lens: one or more pieces of glass, usually curved, arranged to bring together rays of light so they can be recorded on film or paper

light meter: an instrument that measures the amount of light falling on or reflecting off of a subject so the appropriate exposure can be determined

negative: a reverse image (as on developed film) in which shadows and dark areas of the photograph appear light, and in which light areas appear dark

range finder: a particular type of camera that uses a system of prisms and mirrors to bring an image in focus, even though the viewfinder is separate from the lens

rule of thirds: a technique that can be used to enhance the composition of a photograph. By visualizing a graph that splits the viewfinder with two equally spaced horizontal lines and two equally spaced vertical lines, a photographer can place the subject along any of the lines, or where two lines intersect, to compose an effective photograph.

safelight: a light, usually red or yellow, used in a darkroom when printing photographs. A safelight emits enough light to see, but not enough to expose photographic paper.

shutter: a mechanism in the camera that opens and closes to allow light to reach the film

shutter speed: the length of time the shutter remains open when the shutter release is activated. The speed represents fractions of a second.

single-lens reflex (SLR): a camera in which the view seen by the lens is reflected to the viewfinder by a mirror placed in front of the shutter. When the shutter release is activated, the mirror flips up out of the way and the shutter opens to allow light to pass to the film.

stop bath: a chemical solution used between the developer and the fixer when developing film or printing photographs. It neutralizes the developer and helps extend the life of the fixer.

sync speed: the fastest shutter speed at which an electronic flash can be used on a particular camera. Sync speeds vary from camera to camera, but 60 and 125 are the most common.

telephoto lens: a lens constructed so its effective focal length is longer than its actual size

transparency: a positive photographic image, such as a slide, often meant to be viewed by projection

viewfinder: a camera device used for seeing and framing a subject

wetting agent: a chemical solution used to prevent water spots from forming on newly developed film as it dries

wide-angle lens: a camera lens with a short focal length, such as 24mm or 28mm

zoom lens: a lens that can be adjusted to any focal length within its range

Index

albums, 65, 67
aperture, 7, 9, 11, 14, 15, 18, 39, 40, 44, 48, 49
automatic focusing, 12, 14

black-and-white photography, 54-55, 61-63

camera bag, 17
cameras, 7-19; 110 (camera), 12, 16; instant-print, 12; point-and-shoot, 7, 8, 11; single-lens reflex (SLR), 7, 11, 13, 14
careers in photography, 69-70
cityscapes, 47, 49
color photography, 27, 31-32, 51-53, 55
composition, 21-29, 37-49, 51, 54
contrast, 21, 27, 28, 49, 52, 55

depth of field, 15, 39, 40, 44, 45, 48

exposure, 9, 16, 37, 48, 49

film, 7, 12, 16, 32, 34, 45
film processing, 55, 60-62
filters, 18-19, 48, 59
flash units, 11, 32, 34, 35
focal length, 12-13, 57
focusing, 8, 11, 14, 37, 40
frames (for prints), 65-66
frames (in composition), 21, 29, 49

landscapes, 25, 47-48
lenses, 7, 9, 11, 12-14, 15, 18; telephoto, 13, 40, 44; wide-angle, 13; zoom, 11, 14, 57
lighting, 31-35, 39, 40, 48, 52-53
light meter, 18, 32, 34, 40
lines, 21, 26, 28

motor drive, 19, 37

panning, 37

portraits, 39-45; of animals, 43-45; of people, 39-41
printing photographs, 55, 63

rule of thirds, 21, 23-35, 27

shutter speeds, 8-9, 11, 15, 16-17, 18, 35, 37, 39, 45, 57, 58
slide projector, 65, 67
special effects, 57-59

test prints, 63
tripod, 16-17, 57, 58

viewfinder, 7, 18, 22-23, 27
viewpoint, 21, 24-25, 27, 28, 47-48, 49, 55